D1228465

ALL AROUND THE WORLD
IRAQ

by Joanne Mattern

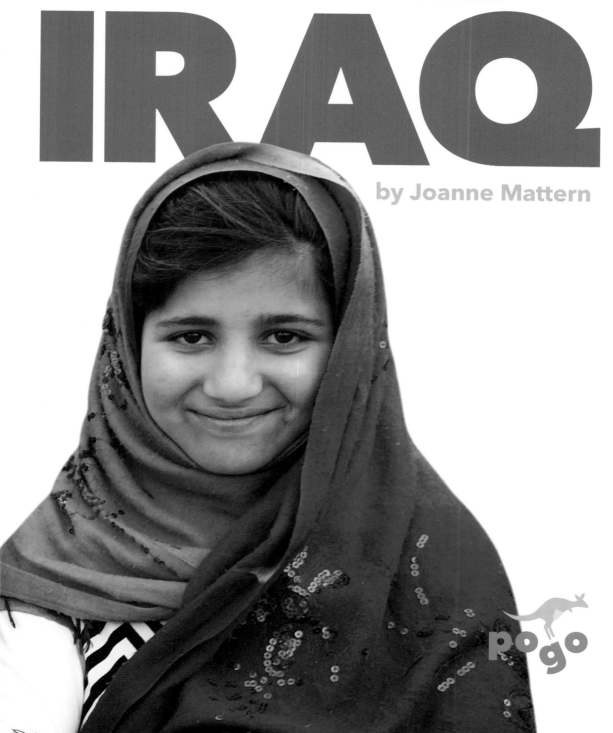

pogo

Ideas for Parents and Teachers

Pogo Books let children practice reading informational text while introducing them to nonfiction features such as headings, labels, sidebars, maps, and diagrams, as well as a table of contents, glossary, and index.

Carefully leveled text with a strong photo match offers early fluent readers the support they need to succeed.

Before Reading

• "Walk" through the book and point out the various nonfiction features. Ask the student what purpose each feature serves.

• Look at the glossary together. Read and discuss the words.

Read the Book

• Have the child read the book independently.

• Invite him or her to list questions that arise from reading.

After Reading

• Discuss the child's questions. Talk about how he or she might find answers to those questions.

• Prompt the child to think more. Ask: The Tigris River is dammed to provide water to dry areas in Iraq. Do rivers flow where you live? How are they used?

Pogo Books are published by Jump!
5357 Penn Avenue South
Minneapolis, MN 55419
www.jumplibrary.com

Library of Congress Cataloging-in-Publication Data

Names: Mattern, Joanne, 1963- author.
Title: Iraq / by Joanne Mattern.
Description: Minneapolis, MN: Jump!, Inc., 2018.
Series: All around the world
Includes bibliographical references and index.
Identifiers: LCCN 2017059273 (print)
LCCN 2018003495 (ebook)
ISBN 9781624969126 (ebook)
ISBN 9781624969102 (hardcover: alk. paper)
ISBN 9781624969119 (pbk.)
Subjects: LCSH: Iraq—Juvenile literature.
Classification: LCC DS70.62 (ebook)
LCC DS70.62 .M38 2019 (print) | DDC 956.7—dc23
LC record available at https://lccn.loc.gov/2017059273

Editor: Kristine Spanier
Book Designer: Michelle Sonnek

Photo Credits: DEA / C. SAPPA/Getty, cover; Ton Koene/age fotostock/Superstock, 1; Pixfiction/Shutterstock, 3; arka38/Shutterstock, 4; Images & Stories/Alamy, 5; Homo Cosmicos/Shutterstock, 6–7; Sadik Gulec/Shutterstock, 8–9; Bulgac/iStock, 10; Marc J Boettcher/Alamy, 11; wacpan/Shutterstock, 12; Xavier Eichaker/Biosphoto, 12–13; rasoulali/Shutterstock, 14; robertharding/Alamy, 15; Ton Koene/Alamy, 16–17; Andia/Contributor/Getty, 18–19; Andia/Contributor/Getty, 20–21; Shutterstock, 23.

Printed in the United States of America at Corporate Graphics in North Mankato, Minnesota.

TABLE OF CONTENTS

CHAPTER 1

WELCOME TO IRAQ!

More than 5,500 years ago, the area of Iraq was known as Mesopotamia. The wheel was invented here! Let's explore this interesting country.

Iraq is in the Middle East. Two big rivers flow through it. One is the Tigris. The other is the Euphrates. These rivers flow into the Persian Gulf.

Tigris River

The world's earliest **civilizations** started here. Towns were built near **temples**. They are called ziggurats. They are made of mud bricks.

Ziggurat of Ur

TAKE A LOOK!

The Ziggurat of Ur has been partially restored. The original structure is believed to have been much taller than it is now.

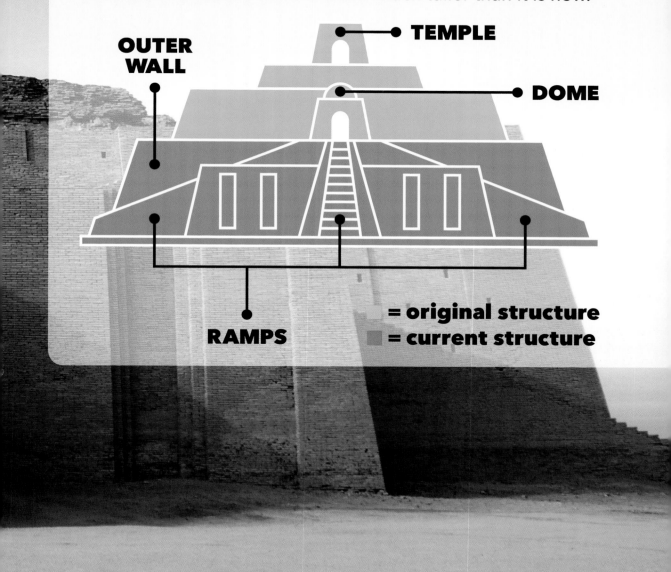

TEMPLE

OUTER WALL

DOME

RAMPS

= original structure
= current structure

purple ink

The people of Iraq elect a **prime minister** to run the government. They elect a Council of **Representatives**, too. The president represents the country at special events.

WHAT DO YOU THINK?

Iraqis dip their fingers in purple ink when they vote. This way they cannot vote twice. How do people show they have voted where you live?

I VOTED

CHAPTER 2

CLIMATE AND CREATURES

Iraq has a hot, dry **climate**. In the summer, it can be more than 110° Fahrenheit (43° Celsius)! A **desert** is in the south.

The middle of the country has hills and **plains**. Mountains in the north are cool and snowy.

Interesting animals live here. The sand cat's paws are covered in hair. This protects them from the hot sand.

More than 400 kinds of birds live in Iraq. Many insects and bugs live here, too. Sun spiders can move as fast as 10 miles (16 kilometers) an hour!

DID YOU KNOW?

Huge sandstorms often happen in the desert. A cloud of sand can be 5,000 feet (1,524 meters) tall!

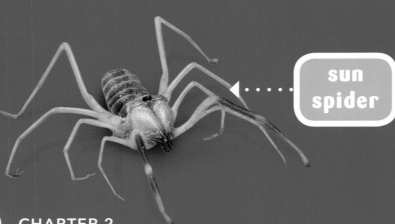

sun spider

CHAPTER 3

LIFE IN IRAQ

More than 39 million people live here. Baghdad is the **capital**. It is also the largest city. Most Iraqis live in apartments in cities.

Baghdad

Some people live in the country. Houses are made of stone or mud bricks. Farmers grow many **crops**. Which ones? Rice. Barley. Dates. They raise sheep.

Many people have **service jobs** here. They work in banks, stores, and restaurants. Others work for the government. Or in the oil industry. Oil is Iraq's biggest **export**.

Mosques are found throughout the country. They are places of worship. Many have domes. Some have towers called **minarets**.

Ramadan is a religious holiday. Families spend time together. Children receive gifts and money.

WHAT DO YOU THINK?

Mosques may have **mosaic** tile decorating them. They may have domes or towers. What features do places of worship have where you live?

dome

minaret

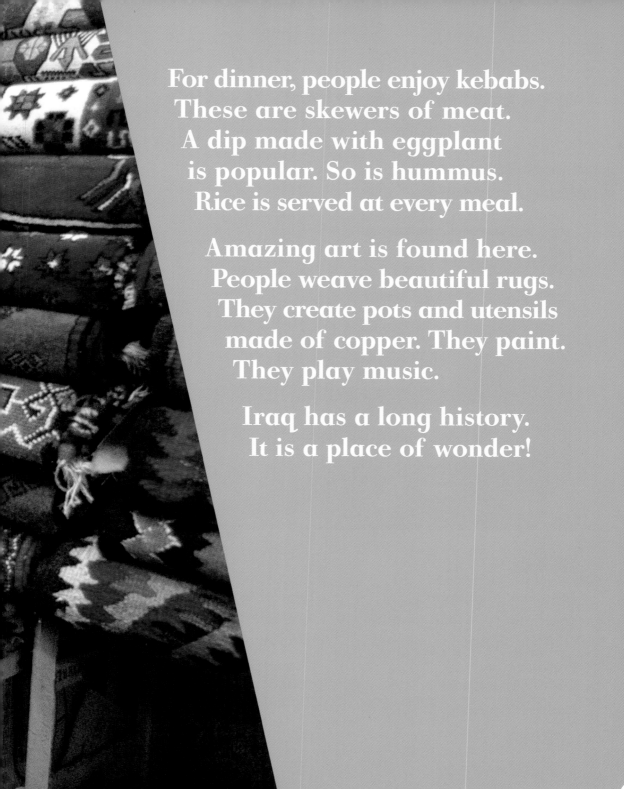

For dinner, people enjoy kebabs.
These are skewers of meat.
A dip made with eggplant
is popular. So is hummus.
Rice is served at every meal.

Amazing art is found here.
People weave beautiful rugs.
They create pots and utensils
made of copper. They paint.
They play music.

Iraq has a long history.
It is a place of wonder!

QUICK FACTS & TOOLS

IRAQ

Location: Middle East

Size: 169,235 square miles
(438,317 square kilometers)

Population: 39,192,111
(July 2017 estimate)

Capital: Baghdad

Type of Government:
federal parliamentary republic

Languages: Arabic and Kurdish

Exports: refined petroleum,
animal products, confectionery
sugar, fruits

GLOSSARY

capital: A city where government leaders meet.

civilizations: Developed and organized societies.

climate: The weather typical of a certain place over a long period of time.

crops: Plants grown for food.

desert: A dry area where hardly any plants grow because there is so little rain.

export: A product sold to different countries.

minarets: Tall, slim towers of mosques, from which Muslims are called to prayer.

mosaic: A pattern or picture made up of small pieces of colored stone, tile, or glass.

mosques: Buildings where Muslims worship.

plains: Large, flat areas of land.

prime minister: The leader of a country.

representatives: People who are chosen to speak or act for others.

service jobs: Jobs and work that provide services for others, such as hotel, restaurant, and retail positions.

temples: Buildings used for worship.

INDEX

TO LEARN MORE

Learning more is as easy as 1, 2, 3.

1) Go to www.factsurfer.com

2) Enter "Iraq" into the search box.

3) Click the "Surf" button to see a list of websites.

With factsurfer, finding more information is just a click away.